Updated and Expanded Edition

The Diatonic Cycle

Essential Exercises
Traditional, and Contemporary Musicians

by Emile and Laura De Cosmo

ISBN 0-634-07940-9

HAL•LEONARD®
CORPORATION
7777 W. BLUEMOUND RD. P.O. BOX 13819 MILWAUKEE, WI 53213

In Australia Contact:
Hal Leonard Australia Pty. Ltd.
22 Taunton Drive P.O. Box 5130
Cheltenham East, 3192 Victoria, Australia
Email: ausadmin@halleonard.com

Visit Hal Leonard Online at
www.halleonard.com

About the Authors

Emile De Cosmo has been active as a teacher, musician, and jazz clinician for over 30 years. Playing woodwind instruments, he has freelanced in the New York area with many noted musicians on television, radio commercials, movie soundtracks, club dates, concerts, and shows.

He is formerly an adjunct professor of jazz improvisation at New Jersey City University, an applied music instructor at New Jersey City University and Fairleigh Dickinson University, and concert/marching/jazz band director at Fort Lee High School, and, along with his wife Laura, feature writers for *Saxophone Journal* and *Jazz Player* magazine. He currently is teaching and writing in St. Petersburg, Florida.

He is the author and publisher of the *Polytonal Rhythm Series*, a 19-book collection that has been endorsed by Paquito D'Rivera, Jamey Aebersold, Denis De Blasio, Slide Hampton, John Faddis, Clem De Rosa, Clark Terry, Bill Watrous, *Friday the 13th* film composer Harry Manfredini, Pat LaBarbara, symphony conductor Gerard Schwartz, Bucky Pizzarelli, Eddy Bert, Dizzy Gillespie, Ray Copeland, Leon Russianoff, and many other professionals.

His performance and recording credits include Sarah Vaughn, Dizzy Gillespie, Dinah Washington, Joe Farrell, Vic Damone, Milt Hinton, Slide Hampton, Bucky Pizzarelli, Gregory Hines, Pepper Adams, Terry Gibbs, Sonny Stitt, Four Tops, and many more.

Laura De Cosmo is an active teacher and professional musician who has worked in the New Jersey and New York metropolitan area playing flute, saxophone, clarinet and singing. She has experience playing in big band, small group, and orchestra. Currently, she is teaching, playing, and writing in St. Petersburg, Florida.

Laura and her husband Emile comprise *The Opposite Sax*, a jazz group performing locally in St. Petersburg, Florida. Along with their recent Hal Leonard publications of *The Woodshedding Source Book* and *The Path to Improvisation*, they also write a weekly jazz column for *The Neightborhood News*.dd

Preface

Just as the color palette is to art, there is an analogous "spectrum" comprised of twelve major keys, twelve harmonic minor keys, and their corresponding chords. *The Diatonic Cycle* is a tool that will enable the student to master this musical spectrum—an essential skill for music students of all styles of music—in a simple, enjoyable way.

Because our personal teaching experience has demonstrated that it is often difficult for a student to become fluent beyond the keys of A major and E♭ minor, and because most methods do not introduce the minor keys until all of the major keys have been learned, the approach taken in *The Diatonic Cycle* instead introduces each key in specific order—which produces immediate results! Each section focuses on one tonal center (key), each of which is introduced using only one new sharp or flat. The relative minor keys are then introduced at the same time, along with each new major key. This approach not only saves time, but relieves the boredom of practicing scales and arpeggios the same way, over and over.

The format used in *The Diatonic Cycle* goes like this: the first key introduced is C major, which contains no sharps or flats. The second key is its relative minor key, A minor, which features one new sharp: G♯. The third key is G major, which contains one sharp: F♯. Next is its relative minor, the E minor, which adds an accidental: D♯. The subsequent key of F major introduces one flat: B♭. Its relative minor, D minor, then introduces one more accidental: C♯. Because of the order in which the keys are presented herein, after playing through six fairly easy keys, the student has experienced all twelve chromatic tones.

The melodic exercises in each section remains the same throughout; however, the harmony and chords drop in and out of the melodic line as the tonal center changes. The rhythms of the melodies change throughout the book as well, which not only increases the student's fluency in playing each new tonal center—an essential skill whether the student is performing, composing, or improvising—but it also makes the execution of the exercises more interesting.

The chord progressions at the bottom of each new section are demarcated by Roman numerals, which indicate the quality (major or minor) of the chord, its root position, and step of each tonal center. Each chord is also labeled with letter symbols: for example, in the key of C major, the I7 is also denoted as Cmaj7, which indicates that it is the chord starting on the first step (degree) of the scale in the key of C major.

After playing through the entire book, the student will have successfully mastered the twelve major and minor (harmonic) keys and increased his or her fluency in playing. Students of both jazz and traditional music will benefit from *The Diatonic Cycle* because it encourages the student to play melodically and rhythmically in all keys.

Laura and Emile De Cosmo

Introduction

The old adage that music is a language is somewhat simplistic. Music is a language, but a complex one composed of twenty-four dialects—variant forms of the standard language. For example, it is necessary for native speakers of the English language to be acclimated to its various dialects in order to fully and expediently recognize and comprehend these variant forms.

Likewise, a musician must be fluent in the language of music and all its dialectical keys. The musical dialects consist of twelve diatonic major tonal centers (keys) and twelve relative diatonic minor tonal centers. A musician must be able to immediately recognize a chord symbol as a "dialect" (tonal center) and be able to "speak" (play) that dialect fluently.

The Natural Gravity of Music and the Cycle of Fifths

In all styles of music there is one basic harmonic urge: the tendency of a tone, chord, scale, or mode to move or fall cadentially to a tone, chord, scale, or mode whose root is a fifth below itself. This natural tendency can be described as a continuous spiral of descending, endlessly falling fifths. It is this cyclical progression of notes, tones, or chords that is defined by and depicted in the "cycle of fifths."

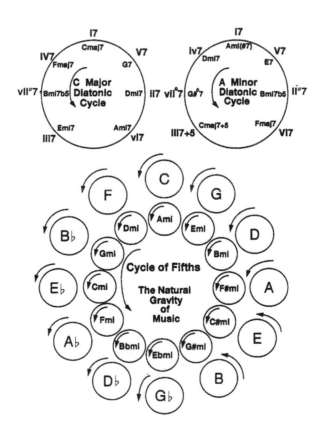

Music's primary progression, the cycle of fifths is also the most crucial for the musician to hear, play, and put into practice. While it is often employed as a means for identifying key signatures, the primary function of the cycle of fifths is to explain the relationships between chords the natural movement between them. But perhaps even most importantly, the cycle of fifths is the key to understanding the most common cadential progression in music: that of the dominant seventh chord (the chord built upon the fifth step of the major or minor scale) moving to the tonic chord (the chord built upon the first step of the major or minor scale), which in all keys is C7, F7, Bb7, Eb7, Ab7, Db7, F#7, B7, E7, A7, D7, and G7.

Within the cycle of fifths there are another twenty-four cycles—dialects moving in the same direction and in fifths—called "diatonic cycles." This term refers to the key or dialectic tonal center, either major or minor, to which each cycle adheres. The cycle of fifths, which encompasses all diatonic cycles, constitutes, then, a musical language.

Progression in the Diatonic Cycle

Normally, according to the cycle of fifths, the note following F would be Bb. However, in the case of a C major diatonic cycle, in order to maintain the tonal center, the F moves instead to a B natural, which is a tritone away from F. This deviation from the normal cycle of fifths to maintain the diatonic tonal center is true for all keys major and minor.

It's worth noting here that, although tritones were generally avoided in traditional music, the momentum produced by the strong harmonic motion of the cycle of fifths was considered powerful enough to justify its use between the fourth and seventh degrees of the scale employed.

The Root Movement of the Twelve Diatonic Cycles in All Major Keys

1. C major: C, F, B, E, A, D, G
2. F major: F, Bb, E, A, D, G, C
3. Bb major: Bb, Eb, A, D, G, C, F
4. Eb major: Eb, Ab, D, G, C, F, Bb
5. Ab major: Ab, Db, G, C, F, Bb, Eb
6. Db major: Db, Gb, C, F, Bb, Eb, Ab
7. F# major: F#, B, E#, A#, D#, G#, C#
8. B major: B, E, A#, D#, G#, C#, F#
9. E major: E, A, D#, G#, C#, F#, B
10. A major: A, D, G#, C#, F#, B, E
11. D major: D, G, C#, F#, B, E, A
12. G major: G, C, F#, B, E, A, D

The Root Movement of the Twelve Diatonic Cycles in All Minor Keys

1. C minor: C, F, B, Eb, Ab, D, G
2. F minor: F, Bb, E, Ab, Db, G, C
3. Bb minor: Bb, Eb, A, Db, Gb, C, F
4. Eb minor: Eb, Ab, D, Gb, Cb, F, Bb
5. G# minor: G#, C#, F×, B, E, A#, D#
6. C# minor: C#, F#, B#, E, A, D#, G#
7. F# minor: F#, B, E#, A, D, G#, C#
8. B minor: B, E, A#, D, G, C#, F#
9. E minor: E, A, D#, G, C, F#, B
10. A minor: A, D, G#, C, F, B, E
11. D minor: D, G, C#, F, Bb, E, A
12. G minor: G, C, F#, Bb, Eb, A, D

The Introduction of Sharps and Flats: POOK

Per the diatonic cycle, sharps and flats are introduced within this book one at a time, and in the order (the Polytonal Order of Keys, or POOK) specified below:

1. C major
2. A minor (add G#)
3. G major
4. E minor (add D#)
5. F major
6. D minor (add C#)
7. D major
8. B minor (add A#)
9. Bb major
10. G minor (add F#)
11. A major
12. F# major (add E#)
13. Eb major
14. C minor (add B♮)
15. E major
16. C# minor (add B#)
17. Ab major
18. F minor (add E♮)
19. B major
20. G# minor (add F×)
21. Db major
22. Bb minor (add A♮)
23. F# major
24. D# minor (add C×)
25. Gb major
26. Eb minor (add D♮)

As demonstrated, the student should follow the POOK order when playing through this study. After the first major key is applied, the student should immediately go to its relative harmonic minor key. (The same key signature is used for the relative harmonic minor, except that the seventh degree is raised by one half step.) The study should be played through all twenty-six keys and in the order indicated.

Influence of the Diatonic Cycle

The diatonic cycle forms the strongest progression of diatonic harmony. The diatonic seventh chords and their corresponding modes present the most basic melodic and harmonic elements needed to begin functioning and developing as a jazz improviser or composer. A student must be able to know and immediately recognize the relationship between a diatonic chord and its related mode or scale in order to produce melodies from either a vertical (chord formation) or horizontal (mode or scale information) approach.

The diatonic cycle progression (a descending spiral of fifths) in all major keys consists of:

- I7 chord moving to the IV7 chord
- IV7 chord moving to the vii half-dim7 chord
- vii half-dim7 chord moving to the iii7 chord
- the iii7 chord moving to the vi7 chord
- the vi7 chord moving to the ii7 chord
- the ii7 chord moving to the V7 chord
- the V7 chord returning back to the I7 chord

The diatonic cycle progression (a descending spiral of fifths) in all minor keys consists of:

- i7 chord moving to the iv7 chord
- iv7 chord moving to the vii dim7 chord
- the vii dim7 chord moving to the III7 chord
- the III7 chord moving to the VI7 chord
- the VI7 chord moving to the ii half-dim7 chord
- the ii half-dim7 chord moving to the V7 chord
- the V7 chord returning back to the i7 chord

It should be understood that the diatonic chords and modes in both all major and minor keys are always of the same species or qualities.

Employment of the Diatonic Cycle

Whether in a major or minor key, all styles of music—including jazz and pop—employ this diatonic flow of chord changes. Composers and improvisers alike add variety and interest to their music by moving from one tonal center to another, thereby creating many different chord progressions. When moving to other tonal centers, the flow of the diatonic cycle may be retained within each tonal center. Therefore, playing this study will accomplish the following:

1. The memorization of the natural sound or gravity of the diatonic cycle for each tonal center.
2. The ability to react to and reproduce sounds heard.
3. The playing of scales, modes, and chords in their natural progressions.
4. Quicker ear/instrument responses, whether reading or improvising.
5. The learning of all keys or tonal centers, both major and minor, with equal proficiency.

Dialectic Tonal Centers or Keys Signaled

The key signature is only a partial indication of the dialectical tonal centers or keys contained in a given piece of music. Novice improvisers and many semi-professional performers improvise in the key of the signature and then rely upon the ear to hear the non-diatonic chords and tonal changes—which many such players are not even aware have occurred. The fact is, chords—other than diatonic chords—from the key being played signal changes of tonal centers or dialects that can be used to improvise.

Popular songs, standards, or any musical composition rarely remain strictly in the tonal center indicated by the key signature, but may in fact change tonal centers several times throughout a given piece of music.

The most common use of tonal center changes can be found in the B section, or bridge, of many tunes following the AABA structure—four eight-measure sections of 32 total measures in length:

1. The A section (main idea), which contains eight measures.
2. The repetition of the A section.
3. The B section, or bridge, (in contrast to the A section), which contains eight measures that are often constructed of two four-measure phrases; the last phrase usually prepares for the return of the A section.
4. The repetition of the A section.

The standard "I Got Rhythm," a song composed in the AABA musical form, passes through several tonal centers during the bridge section by using cycle of fifths chord changes.

Many musicians are aware that a song's chorus and the release or bridge are often composed in different tonal centers, even though the key signature gives no indication of such changes. Too many improvisers, however, are not aware that the tonal centers change within the traditional AABA structure.

Any seventh chord that is different from the diatonic chords of the key usually indicates a change of tonal centers within the song's progression and requires a shift to the tonal center of that key. Those functional chords that, approximately 75% of the time, signal tonal center changes not related to the tonal center of the key signature are: a major seventh chord, a minor seventh chord, and a dominant seventh chord foreign to the key of the tune being improvised.

Chord types from non-related keys that signal tonal center changes are: the tonic chord, IMaj7, the supertonic chord, iim7, and the dominant seventh, V7. In the minor keys, the ii chord is an iim7♭5.

The next common chord in the chain of functional chords is the subdominant chord: IV7. In the minor key, the iv7 is a minor chord.

The submediant chord, the vi7, is the next most common chord, followed by the mediant chord, the iii7, and the leading tone chord, the vii7♭5. These three chords are usually part of a longer progression in changing tonal centers.

After practicing this diatonic cycle study with all its dialectical tonal centers, the student should then commit all tonal centers, with their corresponding chords and modes, to memory. When different chord changes appear in the music, new tonal centers will be readily recognized, and improvising will become easier.

When a piece of music is written entirely within the one tonal center indicated by the key signature, improvisation is easier; but when internal tonal center changes occur, improvisational demands become more complex.

The tonal center approach to improvisational study encourages fluency in the whole spectrum of the language and dialects of music, from which an individual's style can be properly developed.

Standard, Pop, and Jazz Tunes That Use the Diatonic Cycle of Fifths Chord Progressions Completely or Partially in Various Tonal Centers

The following list of standard, pop, and jazz tunes contain the diatonic cycle, either completely or in part. Although it is important to learn the diatonic cycle in all keys and dialects, it is imperative for today's novice composer or improviser to become familiar with the jazz literature that makes use of the diatonic cycle. The more tunes that a student learns, analyzes, and memorizes, the easier it will be to improvise on diatonic chord changes.

- "All of Me" – S. Simons/G. Marks
- "Along Came Betty" – Benny Golson
- "All the Things You Are" – Oscar Hammerstein II/Jerome Kern
- "Anthropology" – C. Parker/D. Gillespie
- "Autumn Leaves" – Johnny Mercer/Joseph Kosma

- "Baubles, Bangles, and Beads" – Forest/Wright
- "Blue Moon" – Richard Rodgers/Lorenz Hart
- "Bluesette" – Jean "Toots" Tielemans/Norman Gimbel
- "Boplicity" – Miles Davis/Gil Evans
- "But Not for Me" – Ira Gershwin/George Gershwin
- "Ceora" – Lee Morgan
- "Chasin' the Bird" – Charlie Parker
- "Cherokee" – Ray Noble
- "Confirmation" – Charlie Parker
- "Countdown" – John Coltrane
- "Cute" – Neil Hefti
- "Daahoud" – Clifford Brown
- "Del Sasser" – Sam Jones
- "Dewey Square" – Charlie Parker
- "Donna Lee" – Miles Davis
- "Fly Me to the Moon" (a.k.a. "In Other Words") – Bart Howard
- "Four Brothers" – Jimmy Guiffre
- "Four" – Miles Davis
- "Get Happy" – Ted Koehler/Harold Arlen
- "Giant Steps" – John Coltrane
- "Good Bait" – Tad Dameron
- "Groovin' High" – Dizzy Gillespie
- "How High the Moon" – Morgan/Lewis
- "I Got Rhythm" – George Gershwin/Ira Gershwin
- "I Love You" – Cole Porter
- "I Remember Clifford" – Benny Golson
- "I'll Remember April" – Raye/DePaul
- "In a Mellow Tone" – Duke Ellington
- "Jordu" – Duke Jordon
- "Joy Spring" – Clifford Brown
- "Just in Time" – Betty Comden/Adolph Green/Jule Styne
- "Kim" – Charlie Parker
- "Ko-Ko" – Charlie Parker
- "Lady Bird" – Tad Dameron
- "Little Willie Leaps" – Miles Davis
- "Loads of Love" – Richard Rodgers
- "Lover" – Richard Rodgers
- "Lover Man" – Davis/Ramirez
- "Meditation" – A.C. Jobim
- "Misty" – Errol Garner
- "On Green Dolphin Street" – Bronislav Kaper
- "Ornithology" – Charlie Parker
- "Out of Nowhere" – Green
- "Parisian Thoroughfare" – Bud Powell
- " 'Round Midnight" – Thelonious Monk

- "Saint Thomas" – Sonny Rollins
- "Satin Doll" – Duke Ellington
- "Scrapple from the Apple" – Charlie Parker
- "Sister Sadie" – Horace Silver
- "Skylark" – Carmichael/Mercer
- "Soon" – George Gershwin
- "Sophisticated Lady" – Duke Ellington
- "Stella by Starlight" – Victor Young
- "Stranger in Paradise" – Robert Wright/George Forest
- "Sweet Georgia Brown" – Bernie/Pinkard
- "The Shadow of Your Smile" – Paul Francis Webster/Johnny Mandel
- "The Song is You" – Kern/Hammerstein
- "Tune Up" – Eddie Vinson/Miles Davis
- "Watch What Happens" – Michel LeGrand
- "Yarbird Suite" – Charlie Parker

As can be seen by the length of this list, a jazz player can acquire an abundance of jazz language and style while simply learning melodies. These tunes, as melodic information stored in the mind's ear, become part of the tonal vocabulary to be incorporated—either in bits or at length—when improvising. For every one of the hundreds, if not thousands, of tunes the astute jazz musician has memorized, they have as many ways in which to incorporate the whole or parts of those songs over endless chord changes. This process, over time, occurs automatically.

Therefore, the novice player should begin to memorize as many different jazz tunes as possible in order to expand his or her improvisational fluency and to acquire a jazz vocabulary and language—both of which should be continuing processes. After memorizing some of the jazz tunes listed above, the student should practice the tunes in as many different keys as possible to expand his or her jazz vocabulary even further.

In order for the mind to fully understand what the ear is hearing, it must be developed. Practicing the diatonic cycle study, along with jazz literature, will develop this facility of the mind to send out to the body that which the ear hears, thus making the musical instrument an extension of the musician's body—and connecting it more directly with the mind.

Enjoy the diatonic cycle, and keep on "POOKing."

How to Use This Book

This book is designed to be played as one would read a novel or textbook. Read through a number of pages and mark the place where you decide to stop. In your next practice session, continue where you left off; continue in this way until the book is completed. This book can be played again many times, thus bringing about results that would otherwise take many years of playing experience to accomplish. Depending on their students' needs, teachers may assign lessons from the various sections as they see fit.

Rhythmic Variation

This book incorporates a number of different rhythms. The variations suggest different possibilities in the rhythmic flow of improvisation and break the monotony of playing ordinary exercises. Playing exercises that are both melodic and rhythmic will refine technique, lead to better sight-reading, and improve playing immediately.

Using a Metronome

In order to maintain rhythmic accuracy and to develop a natural sense of meter, the student should use a metronome when practicing these studies.

Accidentals vs. Key Signatures

Accidentals are employed throughout this book rather than key signatures for the purpose of reading ease and to help the student commit the key signatures to memory.

The Goal of Playing the Exercises

Students should play the exercises in the complete range of their respective instruments with the goal of developing the ability to execute these studies anywhere on an instrument. Also, the student should learn to recognize chordal changes by the sounds of the twenty-four dialects or tonal centers. Accomplishing these things will result in enhanced tone recognition, sight-reading ability, and improvisational fluency.

Tonal Center: C major
Melodic Pattern: Scalar

Exercise 1

Exercise 2

Diatonic Seventh Chords
Key of C Major

Cmaj7	Fmaj7	Bm7♭5	Em7	Am7	Dm7	G7
I7	IV7	vii∅7	iii7	vi7	ii7	V7

Exercise 3

Exercise 4

14

Tonal Center: C major
Melodic Pattern: Arpeggiated

Exercise 7

Exercise 8

FOR REFERENCE ONLY

Diatonic Seventh Chords
Key of C Major

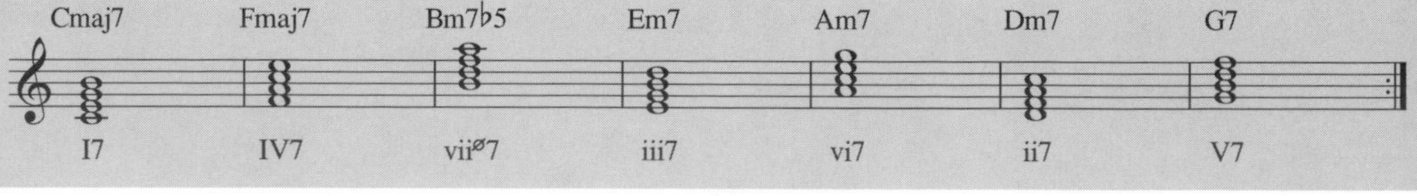

Exercise 9

Exercise 10

FOR REFERENCE ONLY

Diatonic Seventh Chords
Key of C Major

Exercise 11

Exercise 12

Tonal Center: A minor (Harmonic)
Melodic Pattern: Scalar

Exercise 13

Exercise 14

Exercise 15

Exercise 16

FOR REFERENCE ONLY

Diatonic Seventh Chords
Key of A Minor

FOR REFERENCE ONLY

Diatonic Seventh Chords
Key of A Minor

Tonal Center: A minor (Harmonic)
Melodic Pattern: Arpeggiated

Exercise 19

Exercise 20

Exercise 23

Exercise 24

FOR REFERENCE ONLY

Diatonic Seventh Chords
Key of A Minor

Tonal Center: G major
Melodic Pattern: Scalar

Exercise 25

Exercise 26

FOR REFERENCE ONLY

Diatonic Seventh Chords
Key of G Major

Cmaj7	F#m7b5	Bm7	Em7	Am7	D7	Gmaj7
IV7	vii°7	iii7	vi7	ii7	V7	I7

Exercise 27

Exercise 28

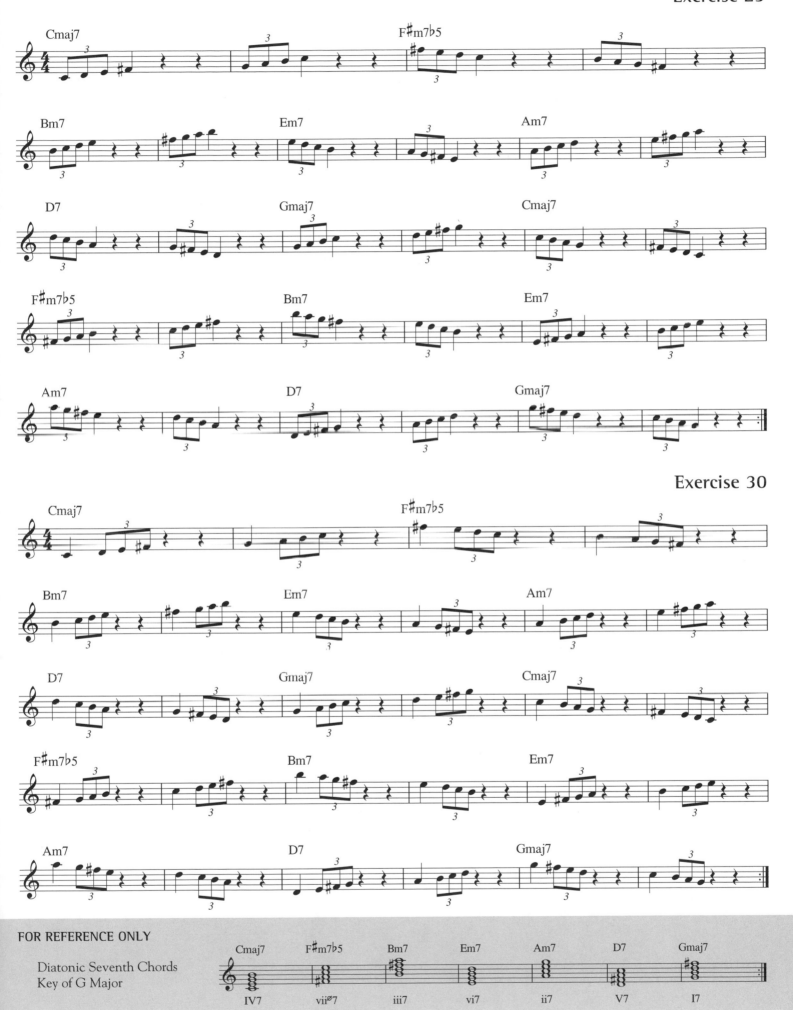

Exercise 30

FOR REFERENCE ONLY

Diatonic Seventh Chords
Key of G Major

Tonal Center: G major
Melodic Pattern: Arpeggiated

Exercise 31

Exercise 32

Exercise 34

Exercise 35

Exercise 36

Cmaj7	F#m7♭5	Bm7	Em7	Am7	D7	Gmaj7
IV7	vii°7	iii7	vi7	ii7	V7	I7

Tonal Center: E minor
Melodic Pattern: Scalar

Exercise 37

Exercise 38

Exercise 39

Exercise 40

Tonal Center: E minor
Melodic Pattern: Arpeggiated

Exercise 43

Exercise 44

Exercise 47

Exercise 48

Tonal Center: F major
Melodic Pattern: Scalar

Exercise 49

Exercise 50

Exercise 51

Exercise 52

Tonal Center: F major
Melodic Pattern: Arpeggiated

Exercise 55

Exercise 56

40

Exercise 59

Exercise 60

FOR REFERENCE ONLY

Diatonic Seventh Chords
Key of F Major

Tonal Center: D minor
Melodic Pattern: Scalar

Exercise 61

Exercise 62

Exercise 63

Exercise 64

FOR REFERENCE ONLY

Diatonic Seventh Chords
Key of D Minor

Tonal Center: D minor
Melodic Pattern: Arpeggiated

Exercise 67

Exercise 68

Exercise 71

Exercise 72

Tonal Center: D major
Melodic Pattern: Scalar

Exercise 73

Exercise 74

FOR REFERENCE ONLY

Diatonic Seventh Chords
Key of D Major

Exercise 75

Exercise 76

Tonal Center: D major
Melodic Pattern: Arpeggiated

Exercise 79

Exercise 80

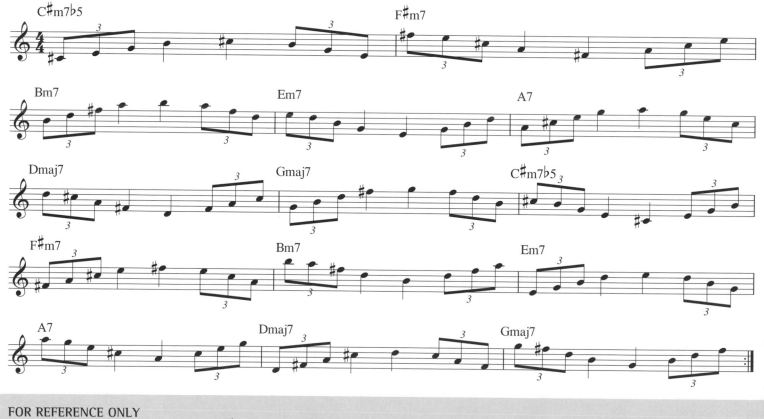

Exercise 82

FOR REFERENCE ONLY

Diatonic Seventh Chords
Key of D Major

Exercise 83

Exercise 84

Tonal Center: B minor
Melodic Pattern: Scalar

Exercise 85

Exercise 86

FOR REFERENCE ONLY

Diatonic Seventh Chords
Key of B Minor

Exercise 87

Exercise 88

FOR REFERENCE ONLY

Diatonic Seventh Chords
Key of B Minor

C#m7b5	F#7	Bm(maj7)	Em7	A#°7	Dmaj7#5	Gmaj7
ii°7	V7	i7	iv7	vii°7	III7#5	VI7

Tonal Center: B minor
Melodic Pattern: Arpeggiated

Exercise 91

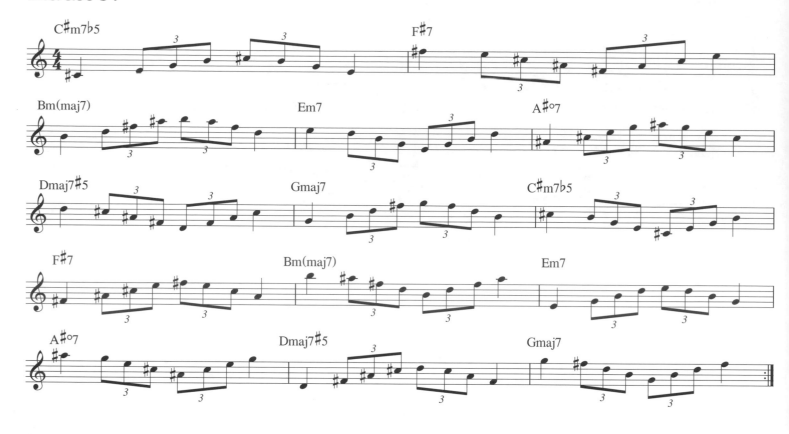

Exercise 92

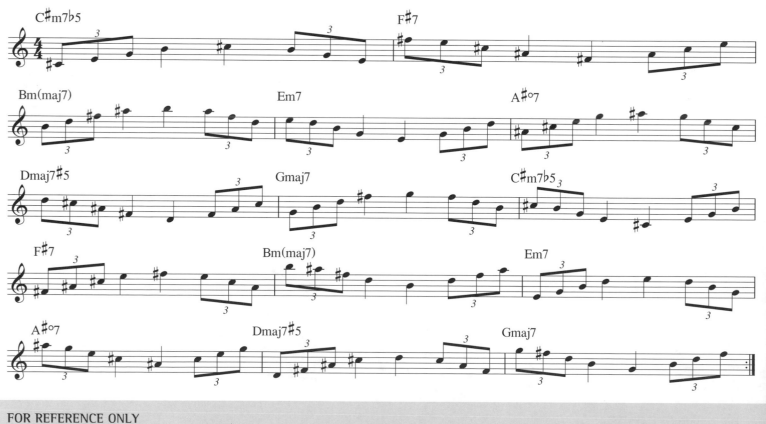

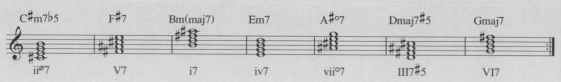

FOR REFERENCE ONLY

Diatonic Seventh Chords
Key of B Minor

Exercise 95

Exercise 96

Tonal Center: B♭ major
Melodic Pattern: Scalar

Exercise 99

Exercise 100

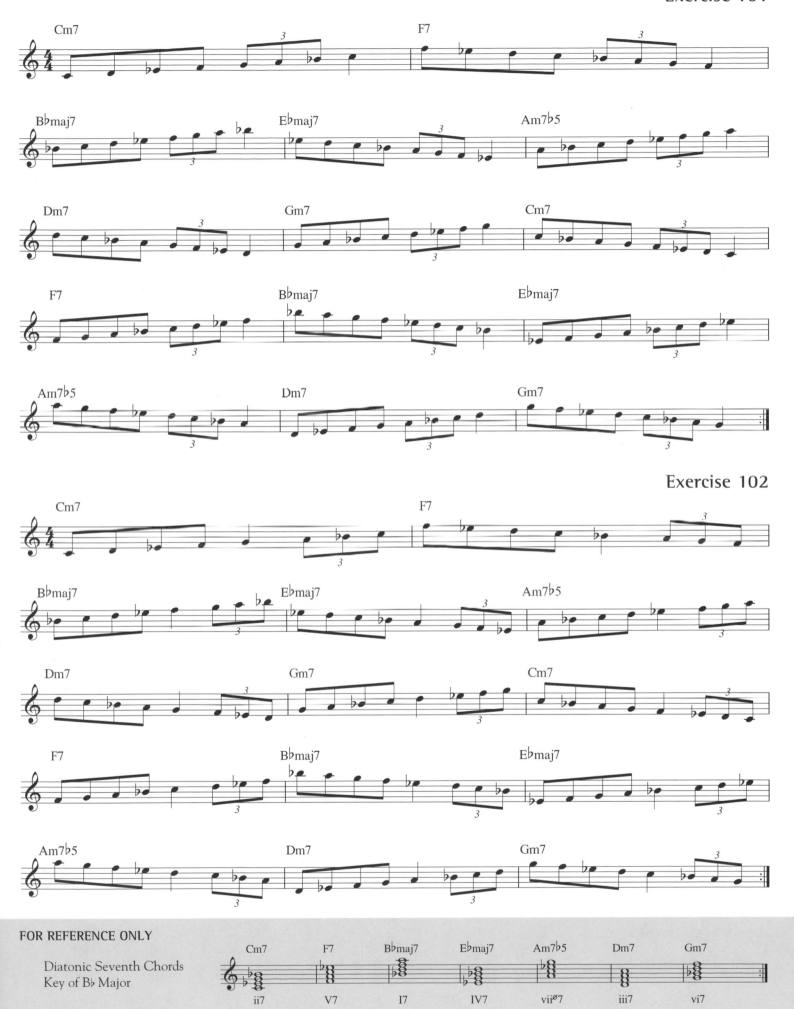

Tonal Center: B♭ major
Melodic Pattern: Arpeggiated

Exercise 103

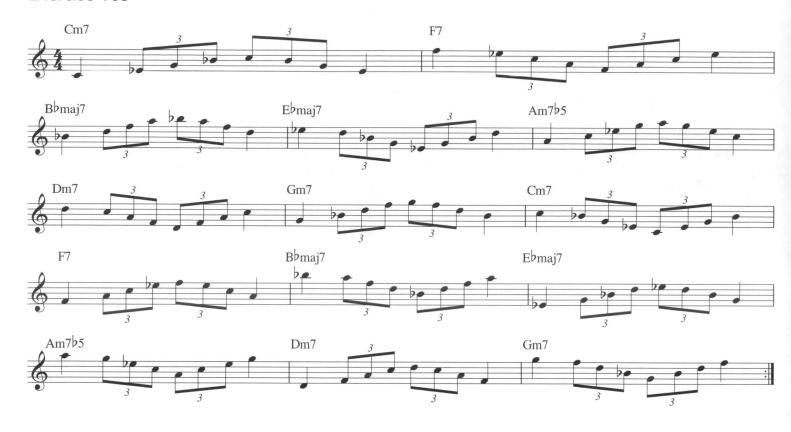

Exercise 104

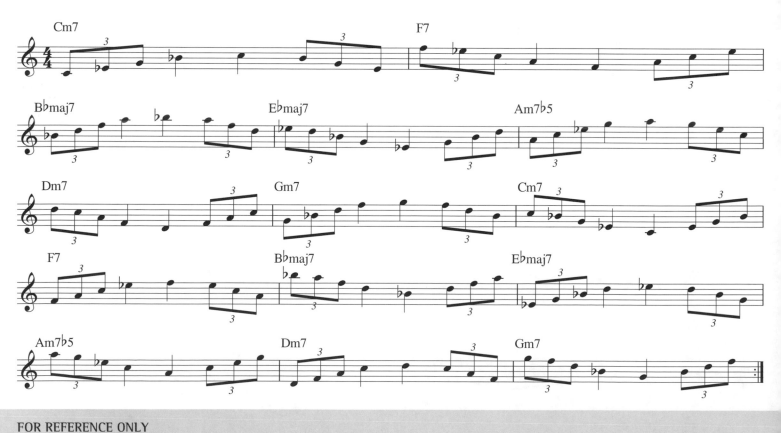

Exercise 107

Exercise 108

FOR REFERENCE ONLY

Diatonic Seventh Chords
Key of B♭ Major

Cm7	F7	B♭maj7	E♭maj7	Am7♭5	Dm7	Gm7
ii7	V7	I7	IV7	vii°7	iii7	vi7

Tonal Center: G minor
Melodic Pattern: Scalar

Exercise 109

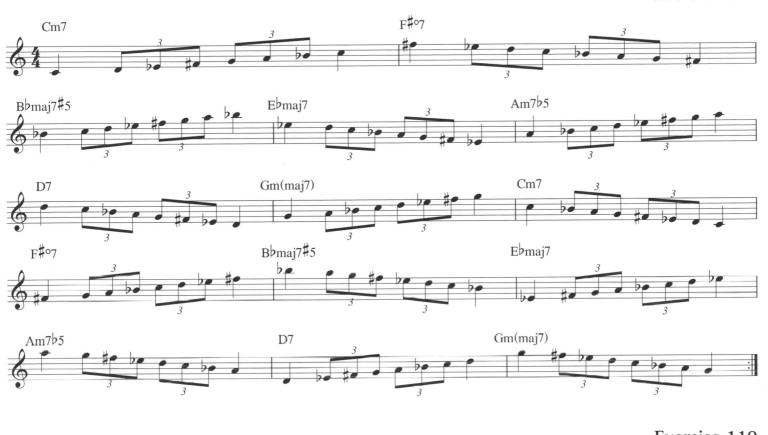

Exercise 110

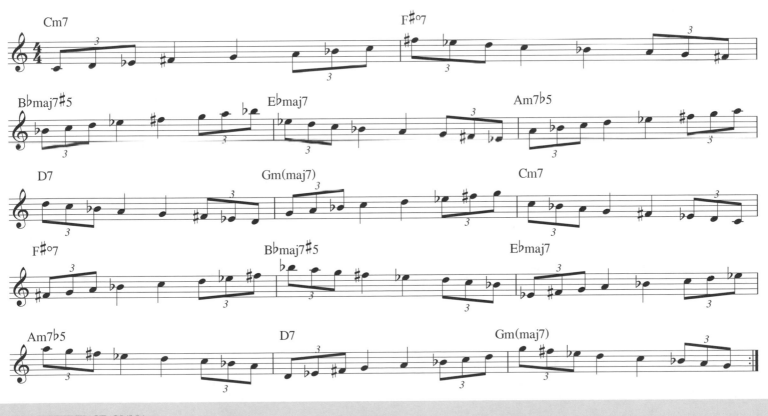

Diatonic Seventh Chords
Key of G Minor

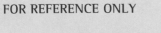
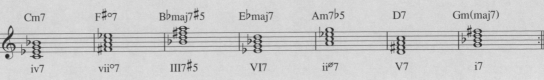

Cm7	F#°7	Bbmaj7#5	Ebmaj7	Am7b5	D7	Gm(maj7)
iv7	vii°7	III7#5	VI7	ii∅7	V7	i7

Exercise 111

Exercise 112

Tonal Center: G minor
Melodic Pattern: Arpeggiated

Exercise 115

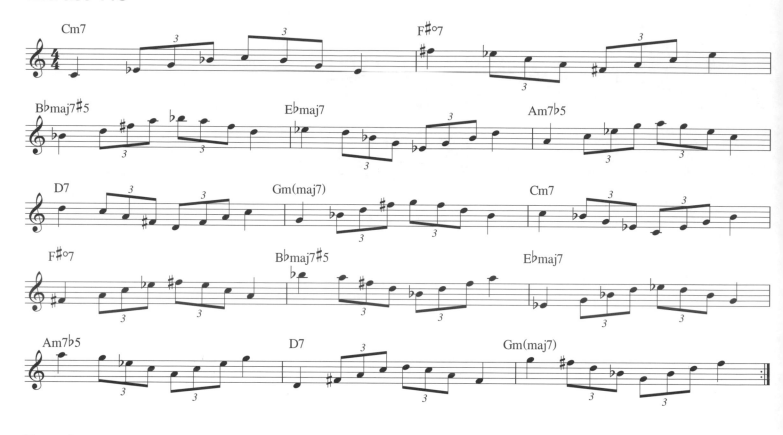

Exercise 116

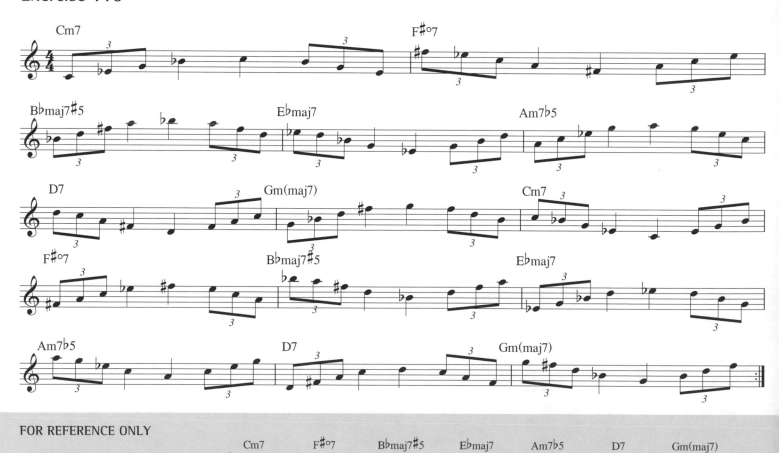

Cm7	F#°7	Bbmaj7#5	Ebmaj7	Am7b5	D7	Gm(maj7)
iv7	vii°7	III7#5	VI7	ii⌀7	V7	i7

Exercise 119

Exercise 120

Tonal Center: A major
Melodic Pattern: Scalar

Exercise 121

Exercise 122

Diatonic Seventh Chords
Key of A Major

Exercise 123

Exercise 124

74

Exercise 127

Exercise 128

Tonal Center: A major
Melodic Pattern: Arpeggiated

Exercise 129

Exercise 130

Exercise 131

Exercise 132

78

FOR REFERENCE ONLY

Diatonic Seventh Chords
Key of A Major

Exercise 135

Exercise 136

FOR REFERENCE ONLY

Diatonic Seventh Chords
Key of A Major

C#m7	F#m7	Bm7	E7	Amaj7	Dmaj7	G#m7b5
iii7	vi7	ii7	V7	I7	IV7	vii∅7

Tonal Center: F♯ minor
Melodic Pattern: Scalar

Exercise 137

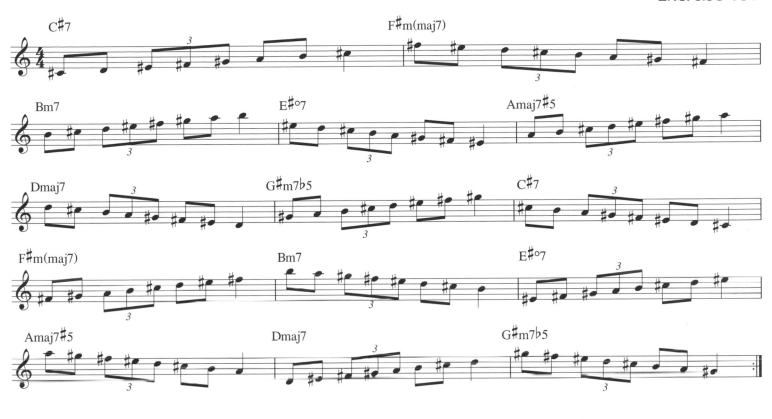

Exercise 138

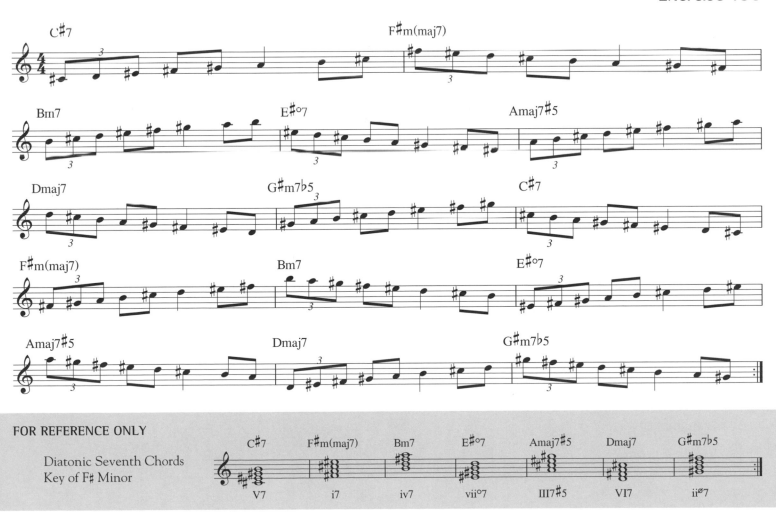

FOR REFERENCE ONLY

Diatonic Seventh Chords
Key of F♯ Minor

C♯7	F♯m(maj7)	Bm7	E♯°7	Amaj7♯5	Dmaj7	G♯m7♭5
V7	i7	iv7	vii°7	III7♯5	VI7	ii∅7

Exercise 139

Exercise 140

FOR REFERENCE ONLY

Diatonic Seventh Chords
Key of F# Minor

C#7	F#m(maj7)	Bm7	E#°7	Amaj7#5	Dmaj7	G#m7b5
V7	i7	iv7	vii°7	III7#5	VI7	ii°7

Exercise 143

Exercise 144

FOR REFERENCE ONLY

Diatonic Seventh Chords
Key of F# Minor

C#7	F#m(maj7)	Bm7	E#°7	Amaj7#5	Dmaj7	G#m7♭5
V7	i7	iv7	vii°7	III7#5	VI7	ii∅7

Tonal Center: F♯ minor
Melodic Pattern: Arpeggiated

FOR REFERENCE ONLY

Diatonic Seventh Chords
Key of F♯ Minor

C♯7	F♯m(maj7)	Bm7	E♯°7	Amaj7♯5	Dmaj7	G♯m7♭5
V7	i7	iv7	vii°7	III7♯5	VI7	ii°7

Exercise 147

Exercise 148

Exercise 150

FOR REFERENCE ONLY

Diatonic Seventh Chords
Key of F♯ Minor

Exercise 151

Exercise 152

Tonal Center: E♭ major
Melodic Pattern: Scalar

Exercise 153

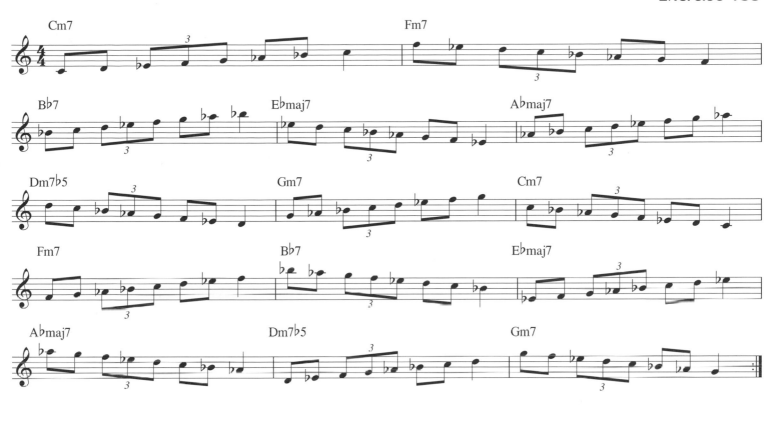

Exercise 154

Exercise 155

Exercise 156

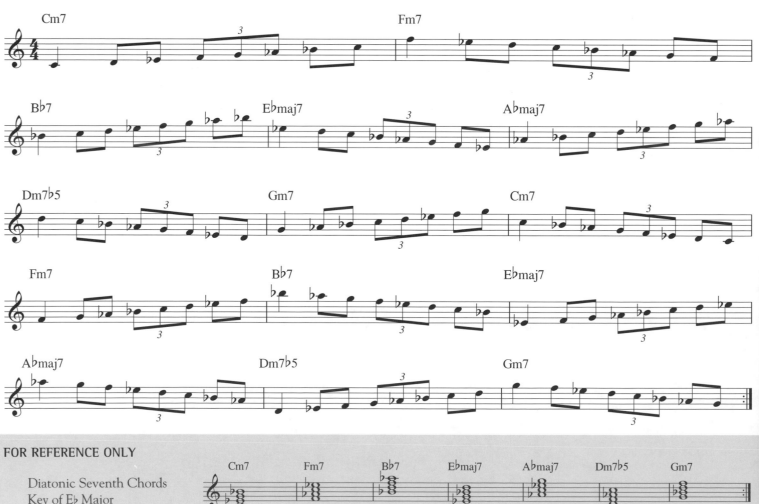

Exercise 158

FOR REFERENCE ONLY

Diatonic Seventh Chords
Key of E♭ Major

Exercise 159

Exercise 160

Tonal Center: E♭ major
Melodic Pattern: Arpeggiated

Exercise 161

Exercise 162

Exercise 163

Exercise 164

Exercise 167

Exercise 168

FOR REFERENCE ONLY

Diatonic Seventh Chords
Key of E♭ Major

Cm7	Fm7	B♭7	E♭maj7	A♭maj7	Dm7♭5	Gm7
vi7	ii7	V7	I7	IV7	vii°7	iii7

Tonal Center: C minor
Melodic Pattern: Scalar

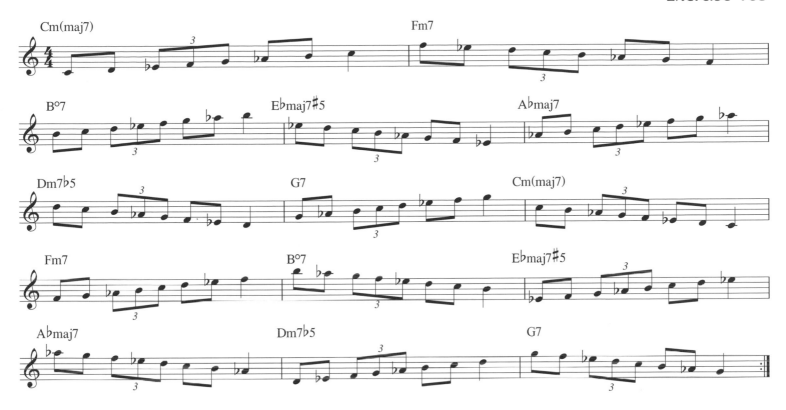

Exercise 170

FOR REFERENCE ONLY

Diatonic Seventh Chords
Key of C Minor

Cm(maj7)	Fm7	B°7	E♭maj7♯5	A♭maj7	Dm7♭5	G7
i7	iv7	vii°7	III7♯5	VI7	ii∅7	V7

Exercise 171

Exercise 172

Exercise 175

Exercise 176

Tonal Center: C minor
Melodic Pattern: Arpeggiated

Exercise 177

Exercise 178

Exercise 179

Exercise 180

Exercise 183

Exercise 184

Tonal Center: E major
Melodic Pattern: Scalar

Exercise 185

Exercise 186

Exercise 187

Exercise 188

FOR REFERENCE ONLY

Diatonic Seventh Chords
Key of E Major

Exercise 191

Exercise 192

FOR REFERENCE ONLY

Diatonic Seventh Chords
Key of E Major

C#m7	F#m7	B7	Emaj7	Amaj7	D#m7♭5	G#m7
vi7	ii7	V7	I7	IV7	vii°7	iii7

Tonal Center: E major
Melodic Pattern: Arpeggiated

Exercise 193

Exercise 194

Exercise 195

Exercise 196

FOR REFERENCE ONLY

Diatonic Seventh Chords
Key of E Major

Exercise 199

Exercise 200

112

Tonal Center: C♯ minor
Melodic Pattern: Scalar

Exercise 201

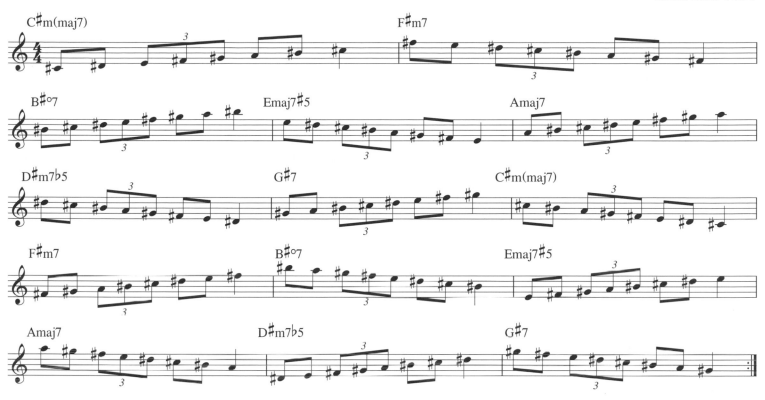

Exercise 202

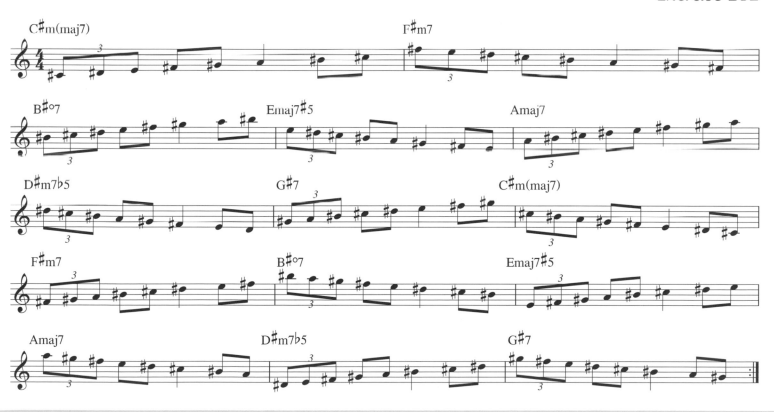

Exercise 203

Exercise 204

Exercise 206

FOR REFERENCE ONLY

Diatonic Seventh Chords
Key of C♯ Minor

Exercise 207

Exercise 208

Tonal Center: C# minor
Melodic Pattern: Arpeggiated

Exercise 209

Exercise 210

Exercise 211

Exercise 212

Exercise 215

Exercise 216

FOR REFERENCE ONLY

Diatonic Seventh Chords
Key of C♯ Minor

120

Tonal Center: A♭ major
Melodic Pattern: Scalar

Exercise 217

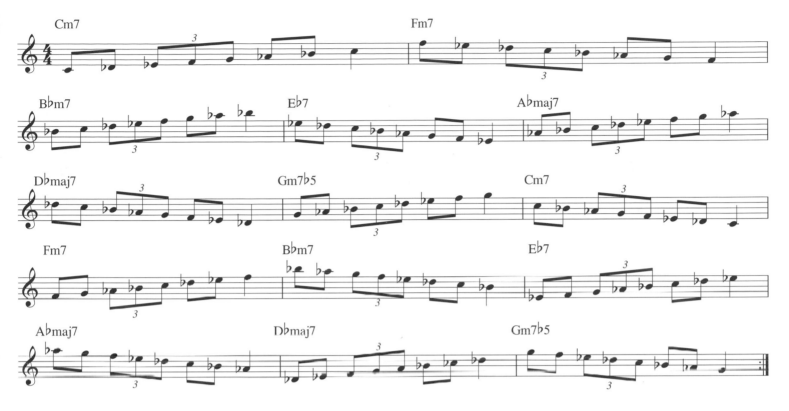

Exercise 218

Cm7	Fm7	B♭m7	E♭7	A♭maj7	D♭maj7	Gm7♭5
iii7	vi7	ii7	V7	I7	IV7	vii⌀7

Exercise 219

Exercise 220

122

Exercise 223

Exercise 224

Tonal Center: A♭ major
Melodic Pattern: Arpeggiated

Exercise 225

Exercise 226

Exercise 227

Exercise 228

126

FOR REFERENCE ONLY

Diatonic Seventh Chords
Key of A♭ Major

Cm7	Fm7	B♭m7	E♭7	A♭maj7	D♭maj7	Gm7♭5
iii7	vi7	ii7	V7	I7	IV7	vii∅7

Exercise 231

Exercise 232

Tonal Center: F minor
Melodic Pattern: Scalar

Exercise 233

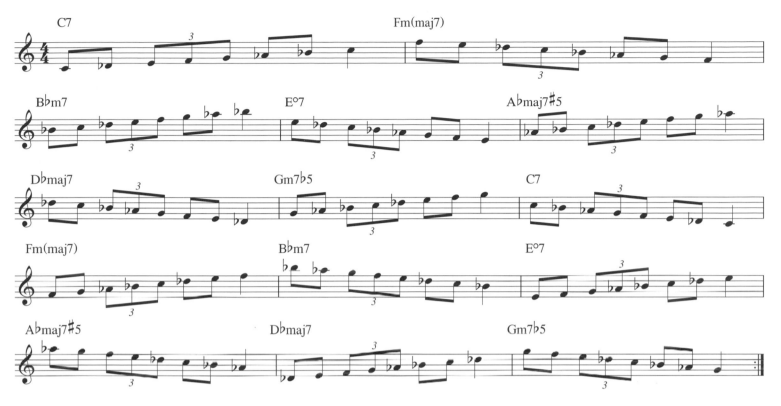

Exercise 234

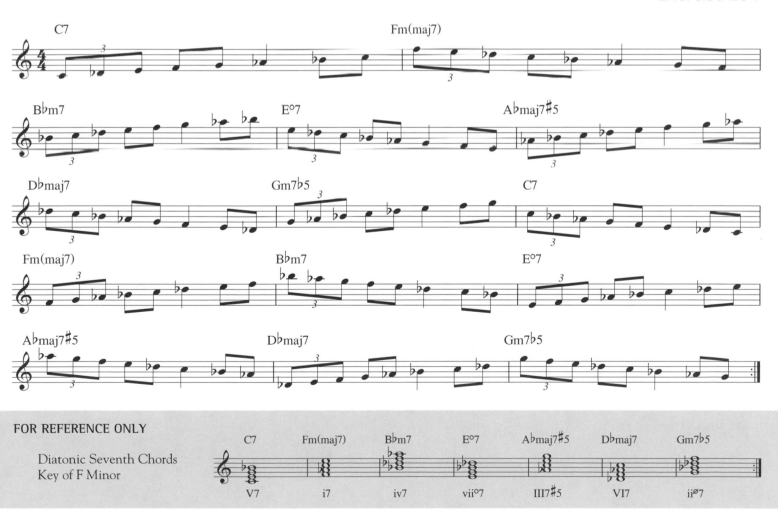

FOR REFERENCE ONLY

Diatonic Seventh Chords
Key of F Minor

C7	Fm(maj7)	B♭m7	E°7	A♭maj7♯5	D♭maj7	Gm7♭5
V7	i7	iv7	vii°7	III7♯5	VI7	ii∅7

Exercise 235

Exercise 236

FOR REFERENCE ONLY

Diatonic Seventh Chords
Key of F Minor

Exercise 239

Exercise 240

Tonal Center: F minor
Melodic Pattern: Arpeggiated

Exercise 241

Exercise 242

FOR REFERENCE ONLY	C7	Fm(maj7)	B♭m7	E°7	A♭maj7#5	D♭maj7	Gm7♭5
Diatonic Seventh Chords Key of F Minor	V7	i7	iv7	vii°7	III7#5	VI7	ii°7

Exercise 243

Exercise 244

134

Exercise 247

Exercise 248

Tonal Center: B major
Melodic Pattern: Scalar

Exercise 249

Exercise 250

FOR REFERENCE ONLY

Diatonic Seventh Chords
Key of B Major

Exercise 251

Exercise 252

FOR REFERENCE ONLY

Diatonic Seventh Chords
Key of B Major

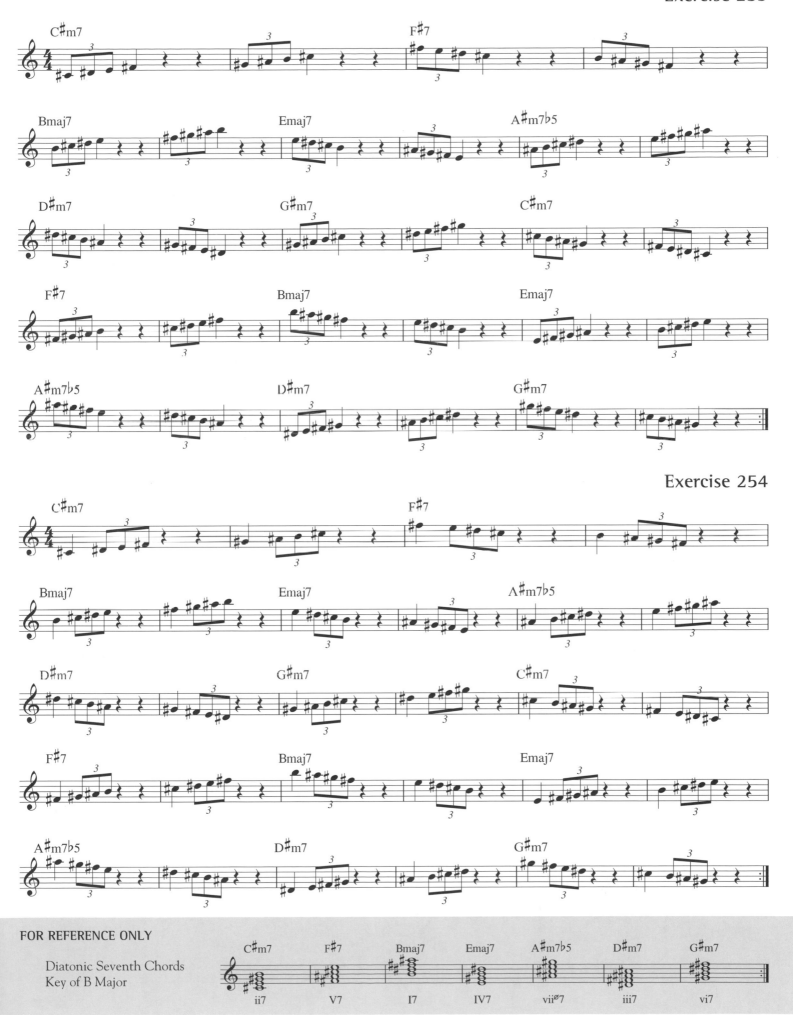

Exercise 254

FOR REFERENCE ONLY

Diatonic Seventh Chords
Key of B Major

Tonal Center: B major
Melodic Pattern: Arpeggiated

Exercise 255

Exercise 256

Exercise 259

Exercise 260

142

Tonal Center: G♯ minor
Melodic Pattern: Scalar

Exercise 261

Exercise 262

Exercise 263

Exercise 264

Diatonic Seventh Chords
Key of G# Minor

Tonal Center: G♯ minor
Melodic Pattern: Arpeggiated

Exercise 267

Exercise 268

FOR REFERENCE ONLY

Diatonic Seventh Chords
Key of G♯ Minor

Exercise 271

Exercise 272

FOR REFERENCE ONLY

Diatonic Seventh Chords
Key of G♯ Minor

C♯m7	Fx°7	Bmaj7♯5	Emaj7	A♯m7♭5	D♯7	G♯m(maj7)
iv7	vii°7	III7♯5	VI7	ii∅7	V7	i7

Tonal Center: D♭ major
Melodic Pattern: Scalar

Exercise 273

Exercise 274

FOR REFERENCE ONLY

Diatonic Seventh Chords
Key of D♭ Major

Exercise 275

Exercise 276

FOR REFERENCE ONLY

Diatonic Seventh Chords
Key of D♭ Major

FOR REFERENCE ONLY

Diatonic Seventh Chords
Key of Db Major

Tonal Center: D♭ major
Melodic Pattern: Arpeggiated

Exercise 279

Exercise 280

Exercise 283

Exercise 284

FOR REFERENCE ONLY

Diatonic Seventh Chords
Key of D♭ Major

154

Tonal Center: B♭ minor
Melodic Pattern: Scalar

Exercise 285

Exercise 286

FOR REFERENCE ONLY

Diatonic Seventh Chords
Key of B♭ Minor

Exercise 287

Exercise 288

FOR REFERENCE ONLY

Diatonic Seventh Chords
Key of Bb Minor

Cm7b5	F7	Bbm(maj7)	Ebm7	A°7	Dbmaj7#5	Gbmaj7
ii°7	V7	i7	iv7	vii°7	III7#5	VI7

Tonal Center: B♭ minor
Melodic Pattern: Arpeggiated

Exercise 291

Exercise 292

158

Exercise 295

Exercise 296

FOR REFERENCE ONLY

Diatonic Seventh Chords
Key of B♭ Minor

Cm7♭5	F7	B♭m(maj7)	E♭m7	A°7	D♭maj7♯5	G♭maj7
ii∅7	V7	i7	iv7	vii°7	III7♯5	VI7

Tonal Center: F♯ major
Melodic Pattern: Scalar

Exercise 297

Exercise 298

FOR REFERENCE ONLY

Diatonic Seventh Chords
Key of F♯ Major

Exercise 299

Exercise 300

C#7	F#maj7	Bmaj7	E#m7b5	A#m7	D#m7	G#m7
V7	I7	IV7	vii∅7	iii7	vi7	ii7

162

Exercise 301

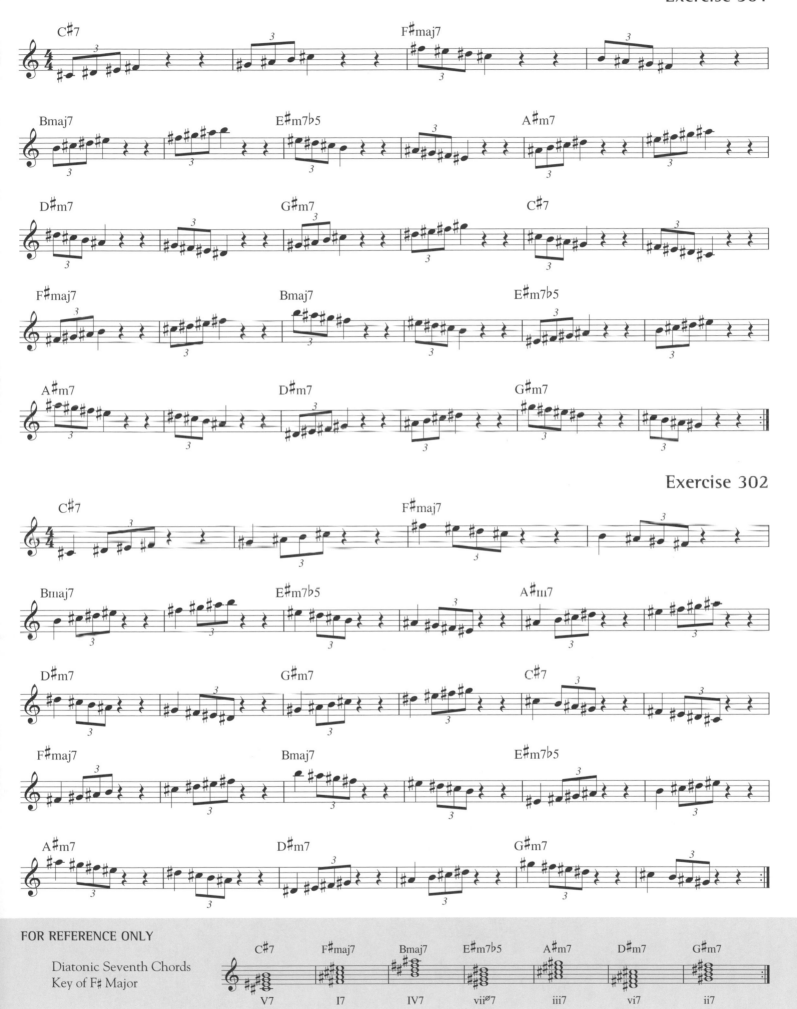

Exercise 302

FOR REFERENCE ONLY

Diatonic Seventh Chords
Key of F♯ Major

C♯7	F♯maj7	Bmaj7	E♯m7♭5	A♯m7	D♯m7	G♯m7
V7	I7	IV7	vii°7	iii7	vi7	ii7

163

Tonal Center: F♯ major
Melodic Pattern: Arpeggiated

Exercise 303

Exercise 304

Exercise 307

Exercise 308

Tonal Center: D♯ minor
Melodic Pattern: Scalar

FOR REFERENCE ONLY

Diatonic Seventh Chords
Key of D♯ Minor

Exercise 311

Exercise 312

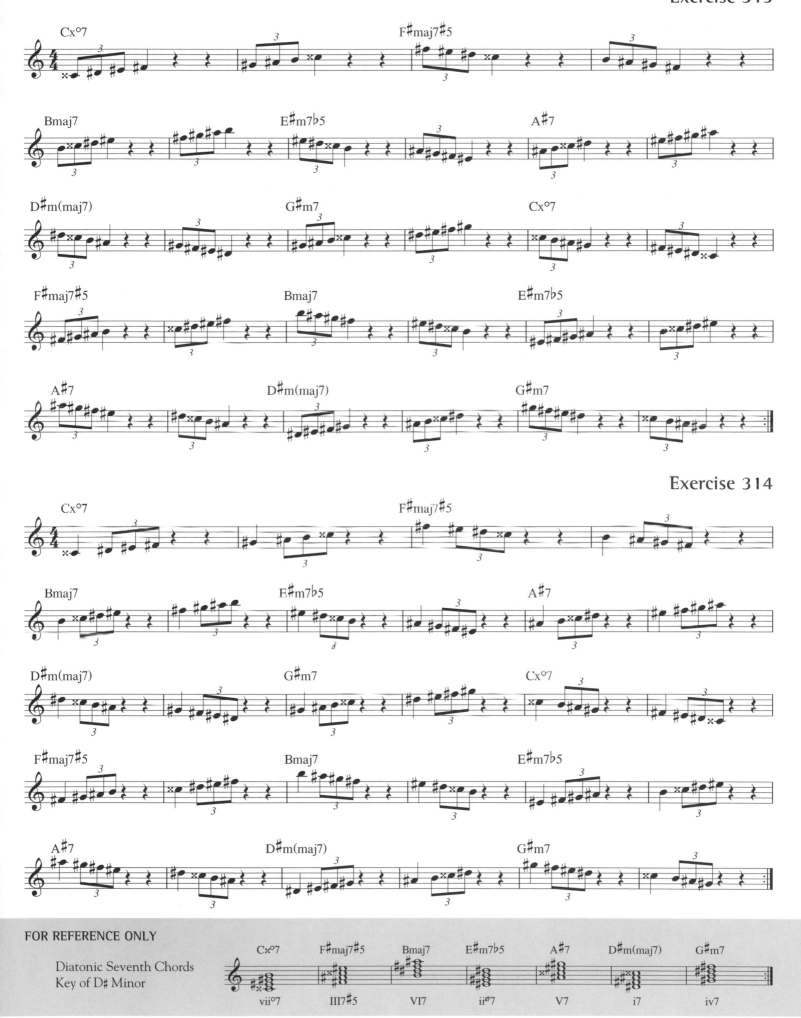

Exercise 314

Tonal Center: D♯ minor
Melodic Pattern: Arpeggiated

Exercise 315

Exercise 316

Exercise 319

Exercise 320

Tonal Center: G♭ major
Melodic Pattern: Scalar

Exercise 321

Exercise 322

Exercise 323

Exercise 324

174

FOR REFERENCE ONLY

Diatonic Seventh Chords
Key of Gb Major

Cbmaj7	Fm7b5	Bbm7	Ebm7	Abm7	Db7	Gbmaj7
IV7	vii⌀7	iii7	vi7	ii7	V7	I7

Tonal Center: G♭ major
Melodic Pattern: Arpeggiated

Exercise 327

Exercise 328

Exercise 331

Exercise 332

Tonal Center: E♭ minor
Melodic Pattern: Scalar

Exercise 333

Exercise 334

Exercise 335

Exercise 336

Exercise 338

FOR REFERENCE ONLY

Diatonic Seventh Chords
Key of E♭ Minor

Tonal Center: E♭ minor
Melodic Pattern: Arpeggiated

Exercise 339

Exercise 340

FOR REFERENCE ONLY

Diatonic Seventh Chords
Key of E♭ Minor

Exercise 343

Exercise 344